DEAR ···

···

···

···

FROM ·······························

©SPIFFY
McCHAPPY

Q. How does a penguin build its house?

A. Igloos it togeher

A jumper cable walks into a bar. The bartender says, "I'll serve you, but don't start anything."

Q. Have you ever heard of a music group called cellophane?

A. They mostly wrap.

Q. What did baby corn say to mama corn?

A. Where's popcorn?

Q. WHAT HAS TWO BUTTS AND KILLS PEOPLE?

A. AN ASSASSIN

Q. WHAT DO YOU CALL A DOG THAT CAN DO MAGIC?

A. A LABRACADABRADOR.

WHEN THE PHONE IS RINGING, DAD SAYS:

"IF IT'S FOR ME, DON'T ANSWER IT."

I'M ON A SEAFOOD DIET...

I SEE FOOD AND I EAT IT.

KID: "HEY, I WAS THINKING ..."

DAD: "I THOUGHT I SMELLED SOMETHING BURNING."

Q. DID YOU HEAR ABOUT THE GUY WHO INVENTED LIFESAVERS?

A. THEY SAY HE MADE A MINT.

I'VE OFFICIALLY RUN OUT OF TOILET PAPER & I'M NOW USING LETTUCE LEAVES TO WIPE MY REAR END. JUDGING BY THE WAY THIS YEAR HAS GONE, I FEAR THIS IS JUST THE TIP OF THE ICEBURG.

"I ASKED MY DAD FOR HIS BEST DAD JOKE AND HE SAID, 'YOU.'"

5/4 OF PEOPLE ADMIT
THAT THEY'RE BAD
WITH FRACTIONS.

WHEN YOU ASK A DAD IF
HE'S ALRIGHT:

"NO, I'M HALF LEFT."

Q. WHY WAS THE BIG CAT DISQUALIFIED FROM THE RACE?

A. BECAUSE IT WAS A CHEETAH.

Q. WHY DID THE OCTOPUS BEAT THE SHARK IN A FIGHT?

A. BECAUSE IT WAS WELL-ARMED.

Q. WHY DO SCUBA DIVERS FALL BACKWARDS INTO THE WATER?

A. BECAUSE IF THEY FELL FORWARDS, THEY'D STILL BE IN THE BOAT.

"HOLD ON, I HAVE SOMETHING IN MY SHOE."

"I'M PRETTY SURE IT'S A FOOT."

Q.How much does a
hipster weigh?

A. An instagram.

Q.How do you make a
Hankie dance?

A. Put a little boogie
In it.

MILK IS THE FASTEST
LIQUID ON EARTH...

IT'S PASTEURIZED BEFORE
YOU EVEN SEE IT.

Q. HOW CAN YOU TELL IF AN
ANT IS A BOY OR A GIRL?

A. THEY'RE ALL GIRLS,
OTHERWISE THEY'D BE
UNCLES.

Q. WHY DON'T SEAGULLS FLY
OVER THE BAY?

A. BECAUSE THEN THEY'D BE
BAY-GULLS!

MY CAT WAS JUST SICK ON
THE CARPET.

I DON'T THINK
IT'S FELINE WELL.

Q. Do you know where you can get chicken broth in bulk?

A. The stock market.

Q. What do you call a fish with no eyes?

A. A fshhhh.

"Doctor, I've broken my arm in several places."

Doctor: "well, don't go to those places."

Just watched a documentary about beavers..

It was the best dam program I've ever seen.

I HATE JOKES ABOUT
GERMAN SAUSAGES.

THEY'RE THE WURST.

Q. WHAT KIND OF SHOES
DOES A THIEF WEAR?

A. SNEAKERS.

Q. There is a new type of broom out. Have you heard about it?

A. It's sweeping the nation.

Q. How did the hipster burn his tongue?

A. He drank his coffee before it was cool.

"I HEARD THERE WAS A
NEW STORE CALLED
MODERATION.

THEY HAVE EVERYTHING
THERE."

Q. WHAT DO YOU CALL A
DEER WITH NO EYES?

A. NO I DEER.

Q. WHAT DID THE DADDY
TOMATO SAY TO THE BABY
TOMATO?

A. CATCH UP!

Q. HOW DO YOU MAKE HOLY
WATER?

A. YOU BOIL THE HELL OUT
OF IT.

Q. WANT TO HEAR A JOKE
ABOUT A PIECE OF PAPER?

NEVER MIND...IT'S
TEARABLE.

WITHOUT GEOMETRY, LIFE
IS POINTLESS.

Q. WHAT DO YOU CALL A
COW WITH NO LEGS?

A. GROUND BEEF.

I BOUGHT SOME SHOES
FROM A DRUG DEALER.
I DON'T KNOW WHAT HE
LACED THEM WITH, BUT I
WAS TRIPPING ALL DAY!

I GAVE ALL MY DEAD
BATTERIES AWAY TODAY...

FREE OF CHARGE.

Q. WHAT NOISE DOES
A 747 MAKE WHEN IT
BOUNCES?

A. BOEING, BOEING,
BOEING.

Q. WHAT DO YOU CALL
SOMEONE WITH NO BODY
AND NO NOSE?

A. NOBODY KNOWS.

A HAM SANDWICH WALKS
INTO A BAR AND ORDERS A
BEER. THE BARTENDER SAYS,
"SORRY, WE DON'T SERVE
FOOD HERE."

KID: "DAD, MAKE ME A SANDWICH!"

DAD: "POOF, YOU'RE A SANDWICH!"

IF I HAD A DIME FOR
EVERY
BOOK I'VE EVER READ, I'D
SAY:
"WOW, THAT'S
COINCIDENTAL."

Q. WHAT DID THE BUFFALO SAY TO HIS SON WHEN HE DROPPED HIM OFF AT SCHOOL?

A. BISON

3 UNWRITTEN RULES OF LIFE...

1.

2.

3.

"WHENEVER THE CASHIER AT THE GROCERY STORE ASKS MY DAD IF HE WOULD LIKE THE MILK IN A BAG, HE REPLIES, 'NO, JUST LEAVE IT IN THE CARTON!'"

Q. WHY DO YOU NEVER SEE ELEPHANTS HIDING IN TREES?

A. BECAUSE THEY'RE SO GOOD AT IT.

Q. DID I TELL YOU ABOUT
THE TIME I FELL IN LOVE
DOING A BACKFLIP?

A. I WAS HEELS OVER
HEAD.

A STEAK PUN IS A RARE
MEDIUM WELL DONE.

Q. WHAT DID THE OCEAN
SAY TO THE SHORE?

A. NOTHING, IT JUST
WAVED.

BICYCLES CAN'T STAND
ON THEIR OWN; THEY'RE
TWO TIRED.

Q. You know what the loudest pet you can get is?

A. A trum pet

Q. Dad, did you get a haircut?

A. No, I got them all cut.

I WOULD AVOID THE SUSHI
IF I WERE YOU.

IT'S A LITTLE FISHY.

I'M NOT INDECISIVE.

UNLESS YOU WANT ME TO
BE.

Q. Did you see they made round bales of hay illegal in Wisconsin?

A. It's because the cows weren't getting a square meal.

Q. Why did the blonde stare at the orange juice container?

A. It said concentrate!

MY FRIEND KEEPS SAYING, "CHEER UP MAN, IT COULD BE WORSE. YOU COULD BE STUCK UNDERGROUND IN A HOLE FULL OF WATER." I KNOW HE MEANS WELL.

SERVER: "SORRY ABOUT YOUR WAIT."

DAD: "ARE YOU SAYING I'M FAT?"

Q. WHY DOES KEEPING TROPICAL FISH IN YOUR HOME REDUCE STRESS AND ANXIETY?

A. BECAUSE OF THE INDOOR FINS.

DAVE JUST GOT TWO NEW PUPPIES; HE CALLED THEM ROLEX AND BREITLING.

THEY ARE HIS WATCH DOGS.

You're american when you go into the bathroom, and you're american when you come out, but do you know what you are while you're in there? European.

Our cleaner told us that she was going to start working from home.

So she sent us a list of things to do.

Q. WHY DID THE COOKIE
CRY?

A. BECAUSE HIS FATHER
WAS A WAFER SO LONG!

Q. WHY WASN'T THE WOMAN
HAPPY WITH THE VELCRO
SHE BOUGHT?

A. IT WAS A TOTAL RIPOFF.

MOM: HOW DO I LOOK?

DAD: WITH YOUR EYES!

I ONCE HAD A TURTLE AS A
TEACHER.

HE TORTOISE WELL.

Q. WHAT IS BEETHOVEN'S
FAVORITE FRUIT?

A. BA-NA-NA-NA

Q. HOW MANY APPLES GROW
ON A TREE?

A. ALL OF THEM.

HR CALLED ME TO ASK WHY
I ONLY GET ILL ON WORK
DAYS...
I TOLD THEM IT WAS
BECAUSE OF MY WEEKEND
IMMUNE SYSTEM.

DAVE NO LONGER SEES HIS
WIFE AND KIDS, ALL
BECAUSE OF GAMBLING.

HE WON THE LOTTERY AND
MOVED TO BARBADOS.

DON'T TRUST ATOMS.

THEY MAKE UP
EVERYTHING!

Q. WHAT DO YOU GET
WHEN YOU CROSS A
SNOWMAN WITH A
VAMPIRE?

A. FROSTBITE

I KEEP TRYING TO LOSE
WEIGHT, BUT IT KEEPS
FINDING ME.

I WENT TO BUY SOME
CAMOUFLAGE TROUSERS THE
OTHER DAY, BUT I COULDN'T
FIND ANY.

Q. WHAT DO YOU CALL A
FAKE NOODLE?

A. AN IMPASTA.

Q. WHAT DO YOU CALL A
BELT WITH A WATCH ON IT?

A. A WAIST OF TIME.

Q. How do you organize an outer space party?

A. You planet.

Q. What's ET short for?

A. Because he's only got little legs.

ATHEISM IS A NON-PROPHET ORGANIZATION.

Q. WHAT DOES AN ANGRY PEPPER DO?

A. IT GETS JALAPENO YOUR FACE.

I AM TERRIFIED OF
ELEVATORS.

I'M GOING TO
START TAKING STEPS TO
AVOID THEM.

Q. WHY DID THE GIRL
SMEAR PEANUT BUTTER ON
THE ROAD?

A. TO GO WITH THE TRAFFIC
JAM.

Q. WHAT DO PRISONERS
USE TO CALL EACH OTHER?

A. CELL PHONES.

IF YOUR NOSE RUNS AND
YOUR FEET SMELL,
YOU ARE
BUILT UPSIDE DOWN!

THE FATTEST KNIGHT AT
KING ARTHUR'S ROUND
TABLE WAS SIR
CUMFERENCE.
HE ACQUIRED HIS SIZE
FROM TOO MUCH PI.

IF YOU SEE A ROBBERY AT
AN APPLE STORE DOES
THAT MAKE YOU AN
IWITNESS?

Q. WHAT DID DADDY
SPIDER SAY TO BABY
SPIDER?

A. YOU SPEND TOO MUCH
TIME ON THE WEB.

DAVE WENT TO A SEAFOOD
PARTY LAST WEEK...

HE PULLED A MUSSEL.

My daughter screeched, "Daaaaaad, you haven't listened to one word I've said, have you!?"

What a strange way to start a conversation with me.

Q. How can you tell if a graveyard is popular?

A. People will be dying to get into there.

I TOLD MY 15-YEAR-OLD SON I THOUGHT 'FORTNITE' WAS AN AWFUL NAME FOR A COMPUTER GAME.

I THINK IT IS TOO WEEK.

Q. WHAT DID THE MOUNTAIN CLIMBER NAME HIS SON?

A. CLIFF.

GRANDPA: I HAVE A
"DAD BOD"

DAD: TO ME IT'S MORE LIKE
A FATHER FIGURE.

TODAY, MY SON ASKED
"CAN I HAVE A BOOK MARK?"
AND I BURST INTO TEARS.
ELEVEN YEARS OLD AND HE
STILL DOESN'T KNOW MY
NAME IS BRIAN.

DID YOU HEAR ABOUT THE MAN WHO STOLE A CALENDAR?

HE GOT 12 MONTHS.

Q. WHY DID THE SCARECROW WIN AN AWARD?

A. BECAUSE HE WAS OUTSTANDING IN HIS FIELD.

I'M READING A BOOK ABOUT ANTI-GRAVITY.

IT'S IMPOSSIBLE TO PUT DOWN!

SPRING IS HERE!

I GOT SO EXCITED I WET MY PLANTS!

Q. WHAT'S FORREST GUMP'S PASSWORD?

A. 1FORREST1

Q. WHY CAN'T YOU HEAR A PTERODACTYL GO TO THE BATHROOM?

A. BECAUSE THE PEE IS SILENT.

Q. WHY DID THE INVISIBLE
MAN TURN DOWN THE JOB
OFFER?

A. HE COULDN'T SEE HIMSELF
DOING IT.

Q. HOW MANY TICKLES DOES IT
TAKE TO MAKE AN
OCTOPUS LAUGH?

A. TEN-TICKLES.

I USED TO HAVE A JOB AT A CALENDAR FACTORY, BUT I GOT THE SACK BECAUSE I TOOK A COUPLE OF DAYS OFF.

Q. WHY DID THE CRAB NEVER SHARE?

A. BECAUSE HE'S SHELLFISH.

Q. WHAT DO YOU CALL A FACTORY THAT SELLS PASSABLE PRODUCTS?

A. A SATISFACTORY.

DID YOU HEAR ABOUT THE RESTAURANT ON THE MOON?

GREAT FOOD, NO ATMOSPHERE.

MY WIFE IS REALLY MAD
AT THE FACT THAT I HAVE
NO SENSE OF DIRECTION.
SO I PACKED UP MY STUFF
AND RIGHT.

I ORDERED A CHICKEN AND
AN EGG FROM AMAZON.

I'LL LET YOU KNOW.

YOU KNOW, PEOPLE SAY
THEY PICK THEIR NOSES...

I FEEL LIKE I WAS JUST
BORN WITH MINE.

AN INVISIBLE MAN MARRIES
AN INVISIBLE WOMAN.

THE KIDS WERE NOTHING TO
LOOK AT, EITHER.

Q. WHAT HAPPENED WHEN THE TWO ANTENNAS GOT MARRIED?

A. WELL, THE CEREMONY WAS KINDA BORING, BUT THE RECEPTION WAS GREAT!

Q. WHAT DOES A VEGAN ZOMBIE EAT?

A. "GRRRAAAAAIIIINN NNS!"

Q. WHY DID THE
CLYDESDALE GIVE THE PONY
A GLASS OF WATER?

A. BECAUSE HE WAS A
LITTLE HORSE!

A TERMITE WALKS INTO A
BAR AND ASKS,
"IS THE BAR TENDER HERE?"

LAST NIGHT, I DREAMT I
WAS DROWNING IN AN
OCEAN MADE OUT OF
ORANGE SODA.

IT TOOK ME A WHILE TO
WORK OUT IT WAS JUST A
FANTA SEA.

SO A DUCK WALKS INTO A
PHARMACY AND SAYS:
"GIVE ME SOME
CHAPSTICK... AND PUT IT
ON MY BILL."

Q. WHY ARE SKELETONS SO
CALM?

A. BECAUSE NOTHING GETS
UNDER THEIR SKIN.

I WAS INTERROGATED OVER
THE THEFT OF A CHEESE
TOASTIE.
MAN, THEY REALLY GRILLED
ME.

SLEPT LIKE A LOG LAST
NIGHT...

WOKE UP IN THE
FIREPLACE.

Q. WHAT TIME DID THE
MAN GO TO THE DENTIST?

A. TOOTH HURT-Y.

Q. WHY DO CHICKEN COOPS
ONLY HAVE TWO DOORS?

A. BECAUSE IF THEY HAD
FOUR, THEY WOULD BE
CHICKEN SEDANS!

Q. WHAT'S BROWN AND
STICKY?

A. A STICK.

Q. WHERE DOES BATMAN
GO TO THE BATHROOM?

A. THE BATROOM.

A POLICE OFFICER CAUGHT
TWO KIDS PLAYING WITH A
FIREWORK AND A CAR
BATTERY. HE CHARGED ONE
AND LET THE OTHER ONE
OFF.

STOP MAKING ME LAUGH.

YOU'LL MAKE ME PUMA PANTS.

TO WHOEVER STOLE MY COPY OF MICROSOFT OFFICE, I WILL FIND YOU. YOU HAVE MY WORD.

"WIFE: WHICH FRIENDS HAVE YOU INVITED OVER FOR DINNER LATER?"

DAD: "MY TASTE BUDS."

Q. HOW DO YOU GET YOUR PHONE DRUNK?

A. YOU GIVE IT SCREENSHOTS.

Q. WHAT'S THE DIFFERENCE
BETWEEN COFFEE AND YOUR
OPINION?

A. I ASKED FOR COFFEE.

Q. WHAT DO YOU CALL
SANTA WHEN HE'S FROZEN?

A. SANTA PAUSE.

Q. DID YOU HEAR ABOUT THE CHEESE FACTORY THAT EXPLODED IN FRANCE?

A. THERE WAS NOTHING LEFT BUT DE BRIE.

HONESTLY, I DON'T MIND LEG DAY AT THE GYM. IT'S JUST THE TWO DAYS AFTER THAT I CAN'T STAND.

A PRIEST RECENTLY HAD A BUG INFESTATION IN CHURCH.
HE SAID, "LET US SPRAY."

I WENT TO A HALLOWEEN PARTY AS THE JOKER, BUT I COULDN'T SEE ANYONE THERE.

IT WAS A DARK KNIGHT.

Q. WHAT DID THE SHIRT SAY TO THE PAIR OF PANTS?

A. WASSSSUP BRITCHES?!

WHAT DID THE PANTS SAY BACK?

DO YOU THINK THAT'S FUNNY, YOU PIECE OF SHIRT!

MOM: "THE MILKMAN
HASN'T COME ROUND YET."

DAD: "HOW DAIRY?!"

BULLETS ARE QUITE WEIRD
INDEED...
THEY ONLY DO THEIR JOBS
AFTER THEY ARE FIRED.

Q. How would you find
will smith if he was
hiding in the snow?

A. You follow the
fresh prints.

Q. Did you hear about
dave? He fell into an
upholstery machine!

A. He's fully recovered.

Q. WHAT DID THE GRAPE DO WHEN HE GOT STEPPED ON?

A. HE LET OUT A LITTLE WINE.

I HAVE BEEN LISTENING TO QUEEN'S ALBUM FOR THE LAST 13 HOURS. I FEEL RATHER ILL.

IT MUST BE THE HIGH MERCURY CONTENT.

Q. WHY ARE DINOSAURS NO
LONGER AROUND?

A: BECAUSE THEIR EGGS
STINK.

Q. WHAT DO YOU CALL A
HERD OF SHEEP FALLING
DOWN A HILL?

A. A LAMBSLIDE.

I TRIED TO ORGANIZE A HIDE-AND-SEEK TOURNAMENT, BUT I HAD NO CHOICE BUT TO GIVE UP.

GOOD PLAYERS ARE HARD TO FIND.

Q. WHY ARE CEMETERIES SO NOISY?

A. BECAUSE OF ALL THE COFFIN.

TEENAGE GIRLS WHO TALK
ABOUT SERIOUS ISSUES ARE
GREAT.
TEENAGE GIRLS WHO TALK
ABOUT GLOBAL ISSUES ARE
GRETA.

Q. WHAT DO YOU CALL A
SAD CUP OF COFFEE?

A. DEPRESSO.

THERE WAS A RIVER THAT RAN
THROUGH EGYPT THAT NO ONE
BELIEVED EXISTED.

LOCALLY, IT WAS KNOWN AS
DE-NILE.

MY BEST MATES WIFE
ENDED UP GIVING BIRTH TO
THEIR SON IN THE CAR!

HE NAMED THE KID
CARSON.

My daughter used to swallow coins all the time as a kid.

I have definitely seen some change in her.

Q. What makes a really good tongue twister?

A. Well, it's hard to say.

Q. WHEN DOES A JOKE
BECOME A DAD JOKE?

A. WHEN IT BECOMES
APPARENT.

MY WIFE ASSUMED I WAS
LYING WHEN I SUGGESTED I
WOULD GIVE OUR PUPPY A
SILLY NAME.

I CALLED HER BLUFF.

My mate begged me to sing oasis's "wonderwall."

I said maybe.

My wife told me to go and wash the car with my son.

I told her I thought a sponge would be better.

I ACCIDENTALLY RUBBED
KETCHUP IN MY EYES.

NOW I HAVE HEINZSIGHT.

Q. DID YOU HEAR ABOUT
THE HORSE THAT FELL
DOWN A HILL?

A. HE COULDN'T GIDDYUP.

(AT A RESTAURANT WITH
FOOD LEFT OVER ON MY
PLATE)
WAITER: YOU WANNA BOX
FOR THAT?
ME: IT'S REALLY NOT
WORTH FIGHTING OVER.

Q. MY FRIEND IS A
FAMOUS DRUMMER. DO YOU
KNOW WHAT HE CALLED
HIS DAUGHTERS?

A. ANNA 1, ANNA 2, ANNA 3.

DAD: "I REMOVED THE WHEELS OF YOUR CAR."

SON: "WHY!?"

DAD: "SO YOU CAN DRIVE TIRELESSLY."

I WON AN AWARD FOR MOST SECRETIVE PERSON AT WORK.

I CAN'T TELL YOU HOW THIS MAKES ME FEEL.

Q. HOW MANY BEERS DOES IT TAKE TO GET A BIRD DRUNK?

A. TOUCANS.

OH NO, I'VE JUST BURNT MY HAWAIIAN PIZZA!

I SHOULD HAVE LISTED TO MY WIFE AND PUT IT ON ALOHA TEMPERATURE.

THE EARLIEST MEMORY I
HAVE AS A CHILD IS
VISITING THE OPTICIAN AND
GETTING MY GLASSES.

LIFE BEFORE THAT WAS A
BIT OF A BLUR.

WE HAVE A PRINTER AT
WORK THAT WE HAVE
NICKNAMED BOB MARLEY.

IT'S ALWAYS 'JAMMIN.'

MY WIFE KEEPS TELLING
ME TO STOP PRETENDING
TO BE BUTTER.

BUT I'M ON A ROLL NOW.

Q. DID I TELL YOU I
USED TO HAVE A JOB
COLLECTING LEAVES?

A. I WAS RAKING IT IN.

ASTRONOMERS WERE BORED
& TIRED AFTER WATCHING
THE MOON GO AROUND THE
EARTH FOR 24 HOURS, SO
THEY CALLED IT A DAY.

MY MATE DAVE LOST HIS
ID WHEN WE WENT OUT
LAST FRIDAY.

SO NOW I CALL HIM DAV.

TWO PEANUTS WERE
WALKING DOWN THE
STREET.

ONE WAS SALTED.

Q. DID YOU HEAR ABOUT
THE KIDNAPPING AT
SCHOOL?

A. HE WOKE UP.

Q. WHAT DOES A BABY
COMPUTER CALL HIS
FATHER?

A. DATA.

Q. WHY ARE ELEVATOR
JOKES SO GOOD?

A. THEY WORK ON SO MANY
LEVELS.

I DON'T TRUST STAIRS.

THEY'RE ALWAYS UP TO
SOMETHING.

Q. WHAT DO YOU CALL A
SMALL MOTHER?

A. A MINIMUM.

Q. WHAT DID ONE AVOCADO
HALF SAY TO THE OTHER?

A. "WITHOUT YOU, I'M
EMPTY INSIDE!"

MY BOSS TOLD ME TO
HAVE A GOOD DAY...

SO I WENT HOME.

I AM ONLY A SOCIAL VEGAN.

I AVOID MEET.

Q. HAVE YOU HEARD
ABOUT THAT MOVIE,
CONSTIPATION?

A. THAT'S BECAUSE IT
HASN'T COME OUT YET.

Q. HAVE YOU EVER TRIED
TO EAT A CLOCK?

A. IT'S REALLY TIME
CONSUMING.

Q.DID YOU HEAR THAT
RUMOR ABOUT WHAT THE
BUTTER DID?

A. I'M NOT GOING TO
SPREAD IT!

RIP
Boiled water.

You will be mist.

I wrote a song all about tortillas.

Come to think of it, it's actually more of a wrap.

I HONESTLY DIDN'T THINK THAT MY FATHER WOULD STEAL FROM HIS JOB AS A ROAD WORKER...

BUT WHEN I GOT HOME, ALL THE SIGNS WERE THERE.

I JUST WANT TO GIVE A BIG SHOUT-OUT TO ALL THE SIDEWALKS FOR KEEPING ME OFF THE STREETS!

Q. WHAT DID THE NUT SAY WHEN IT WAS CHASING THE OTHER NUT?

A. I'M A CASHEW.

Q. CAN YOU NAME ONE PERFUME COMMERCIAL THAT MAKES ANY SENSE?

A. OF COURSE, THEY ALL MAKE SCENTS!

IT TOOK ME 11 PUNS FOR MY
WIFE TO FINALLY LAUGH...

BECAUSE NO PUN IN TEN
DID.

I TRIED SUING BRITISH
AIRWAYS AFTER THEY
MISPLACED MY LUGGAGE.

I LOST MY CASE.

Q. WHAT DO YOU CALL A JANITOR WHO IS ALWAYS SMOKING WEED?

A. HIGH MAINTENANCE.

Q. WHY DOES SNOOP DOGG ALWAYS HAVE TO CARRY AN UMBRELLA?

A. FO' DRIZZLE.

I HAD AN OUT-OF-BODY
EXPERIENCE LAST WEEK.

I WAS BESIDE MYSELF.

MY THERAPIST HATES THAT
I STAND IN THE CORNER OF
THE WAITING ROOM,
BLOWING AIR AT EVERYONE...
IT'S ANNOYING, BUT I'M A
BIG FAN.

***Side effects of reading this book include laughter, eye rolls, eye pokes(self-inflicted), eye spasms, confusion, happiness, joy, on occasion, ecstasy. Avoid prolonged exposure to this book. Use as directed. Do not read this book while operating a vehicle or heavy machinery. Any resemblance between this book and other crappy bad joke books is purely coincidental. This book may contain nuts, but we doubt it.

PLEASE CONSIDER LEAVING A REVIEW FOR THIS BOOK OF EXCEPTIONALLY BAD DAD JOKES.

THANKS A LATTE!

VOLUME TWO IS OUT NOW!

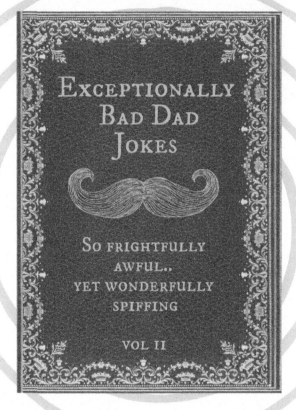

EXCEPTIONALLY
BAD DAD
JOKES

SO FRIGHTFULLY
AWFUL..
YET WONDERFULLY
SPIFFING

VOL II

ISBN-13 : 979-8691550928

amazon

Made in the USA
Monee, IL
14 December 2022